DESIGN YO
WORKBOOK

Male
(Front)

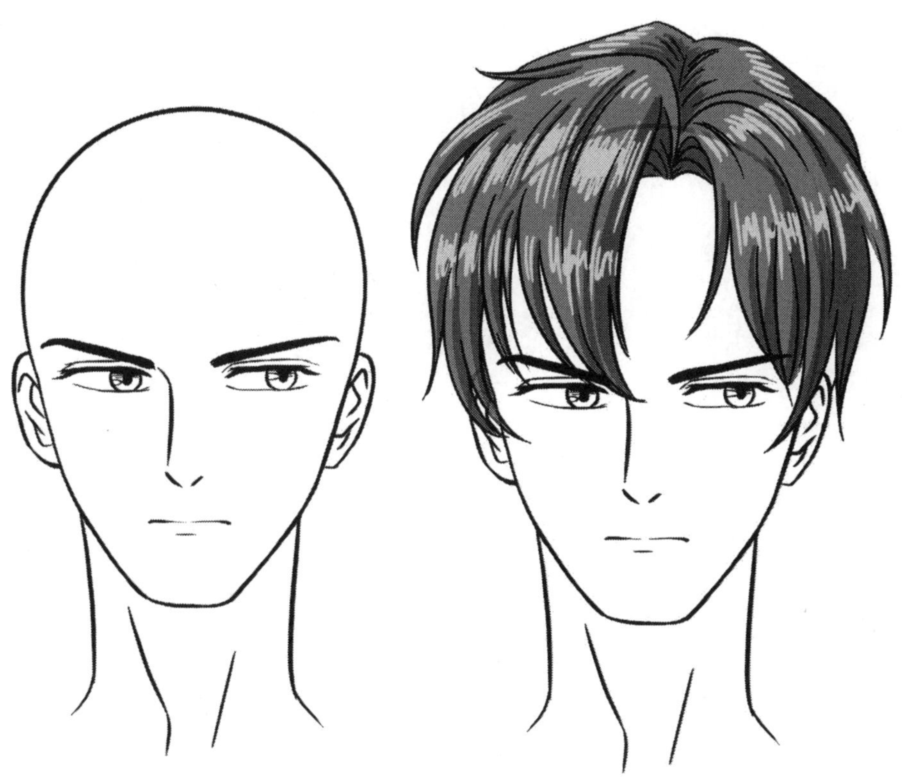

Mei Yu
Artist on YouTube
Over 300 Million Views

Hi, creative fans and new friends!

I'm Mei Yu, a popular artist on YouTube. My channel has 800+ art videos and animations, over 300 million views, and 1.5 million subscribers at: www.youtube.com/MeiYu

I hope you have lots of fun drawing and coloring hairstyles in this WorkBook while using my eBook **Draw 1 Boy with 20 Hairstyles** as your guide.

I created this WorkBook to help you get started easy, and to practice more. You'll use the same head template that I used when I designed the hairstyles from my eBook. There are 20 of them for the 20 hairstyles. I also provided 10 bonus templates for you to practice or to create your own hair designs!

Please share photos of your drawings on the Amazon review section for this book, on social media using #MeiYuArt, and with your friends and family. I'd love to see what you come up with!

Happy Drawing!

Mei Yu

Design Your Hair WorkBook: Male (Front)
Paperback ISBN: 978-1-989939-46-8
First Published December 2020
Book design, cover design, text, and illustrations by Mei Yu.
For business inquiries, please contact the author.

The Apple logo and iBooks are trademarks of Apple Inc., registered in the U.S. and other countries. App Store is a service mark of Apple Inc. Amazon, Kindle, and all related logos are trademarks of Amazon.com, Inc. or its affiliates.
Android is a trademark of Google LLC.

Use this eBook as your guide

TIPS Before You Start:

1. Put a few sheets of copy paper under each page you're drawing and coloring on if you're using markers, to help prevent ink from seeping through onto the next image.

2. Use art supplies like crayons, markers, gel pens, and colored pencils.

3. Try not to apply too many layers or put too much pressure on the page. Easy does it. Happy Drawing!

This book is dedicated to you!

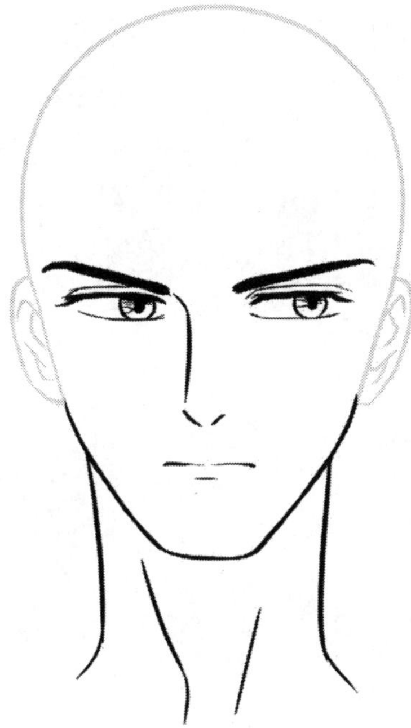

Hairstyle 1:
Hair in Eyes

DESIGN YOUR HAIR WORKBOOK: Male (Front)
by Mei Yu

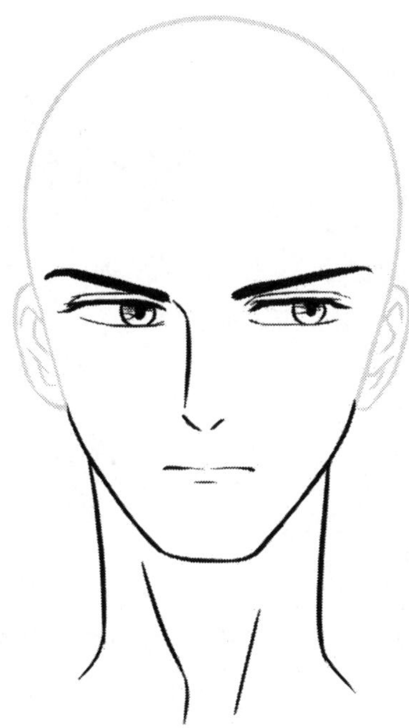

Hairstyle 2:
Stylishly Twisted

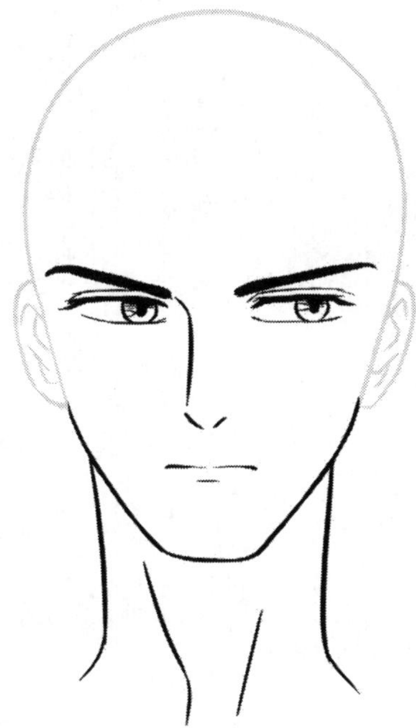

Hairstyle 3:
Messy Spikes

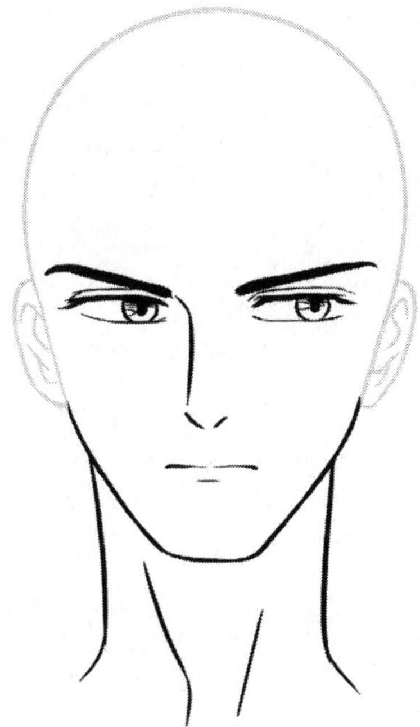

Hairstyle 4:
Long + Loose

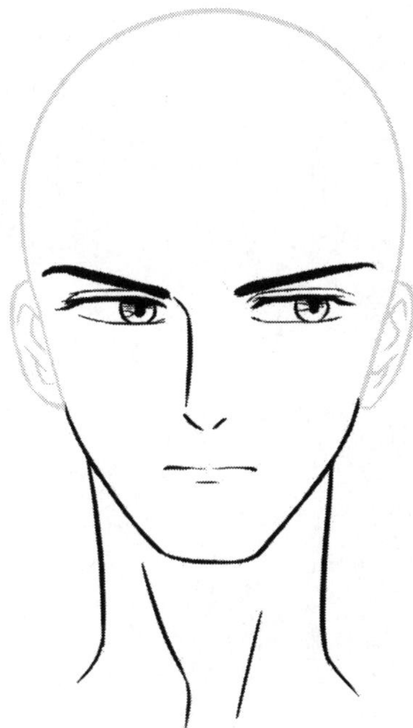

DESIGN YOUR HAIR WORKBOOK: Male (Front)
by Mei Yu

Hairstyle 5:
K-pop Inspired

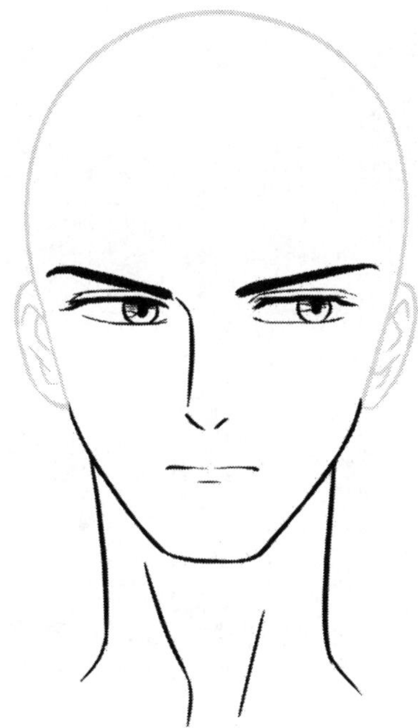

Hairstyle 6:
Giant and Poofy

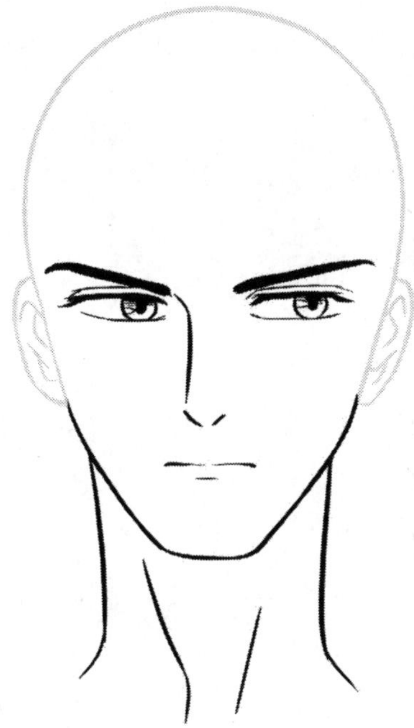

Hairstyle 7:
Short + Choppy

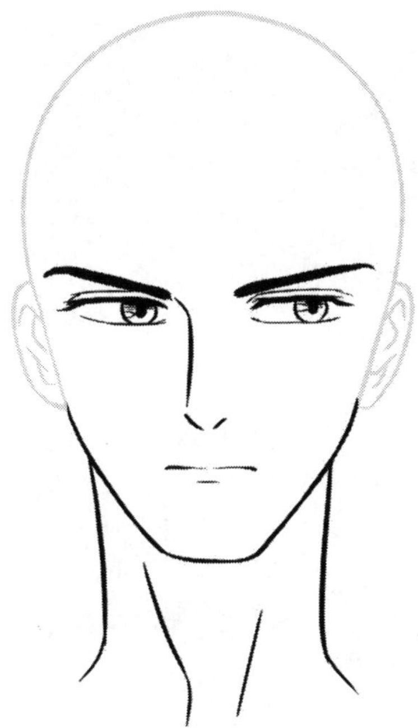

DESIGN YOUR HAIR WORKBOOK: Male (Front)
by Mei Yu

Hairstyle 8:
Wavy Hair

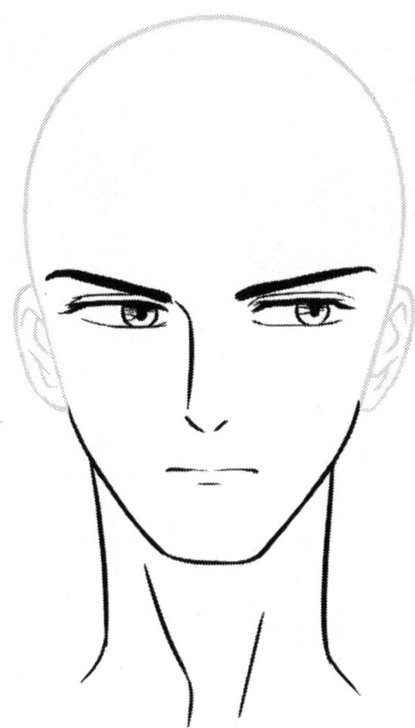

Hairstyle 9:
Front Spikes

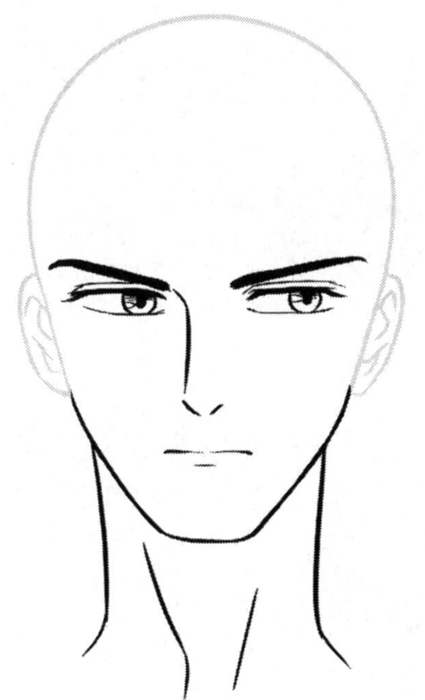

Hairstyle 10:
Wild Anime Hair

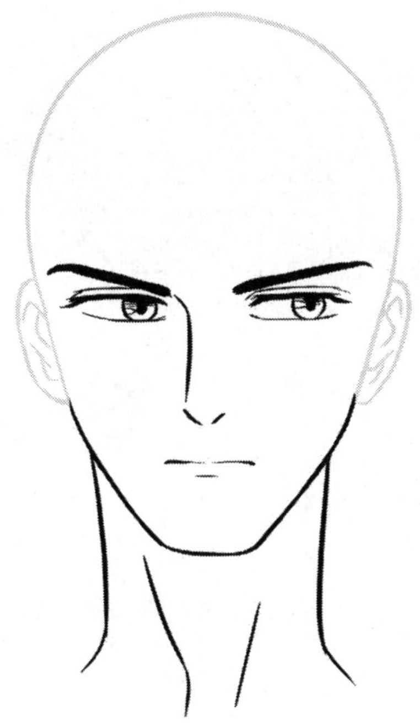

Hairstyle 11:
Wide Spikes

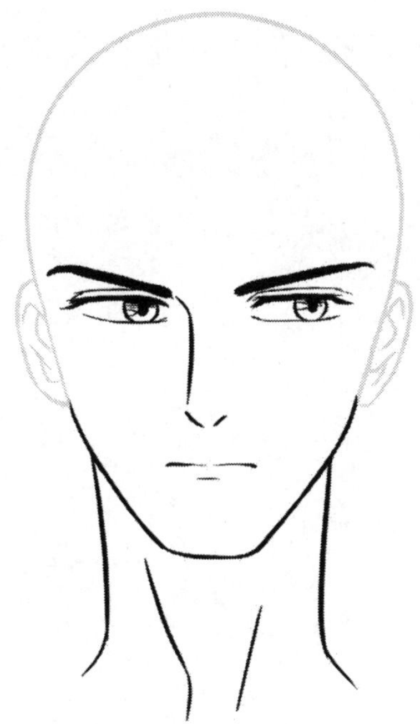

Hairstyle 12:
Cute Swept Hair

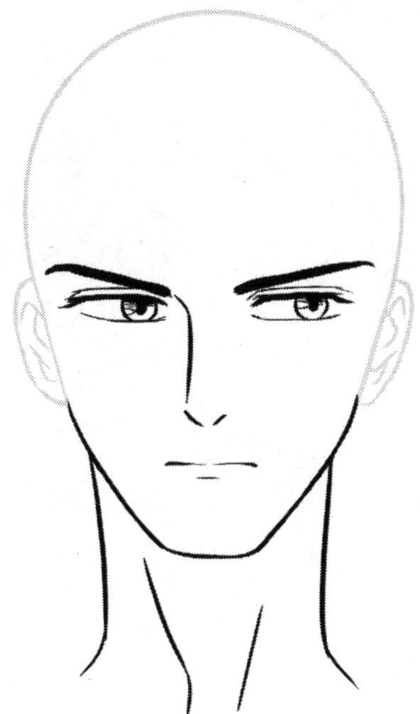

Hairstyle 13:
Mohawk

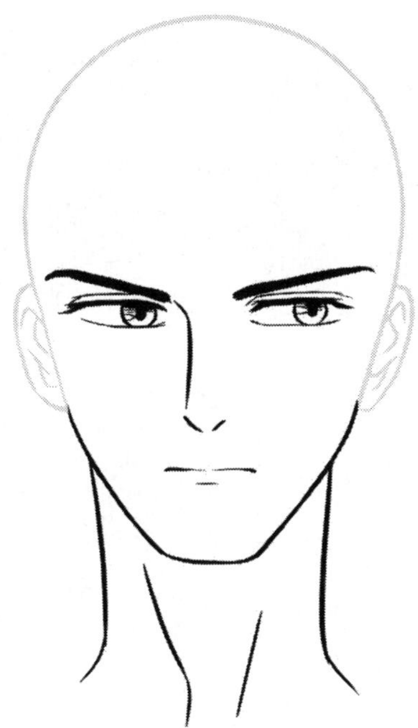

Hairstyle 14:
Shaggy Hair

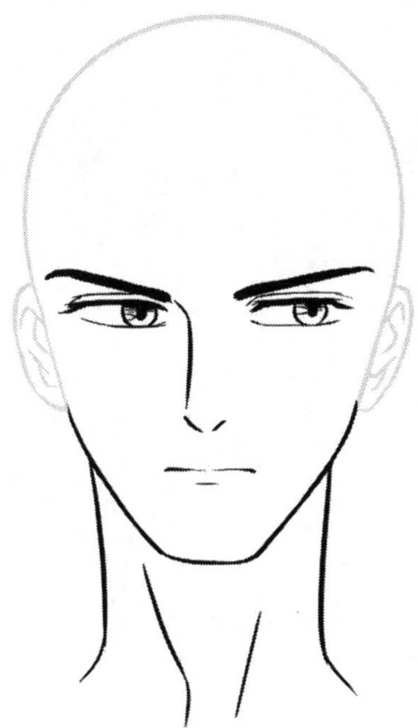

Hairstyle 15:
Man Bun

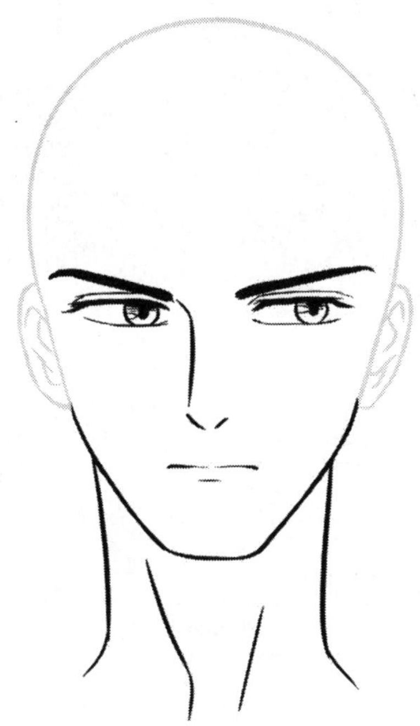

Hairstyle 16:
Parted Bangs

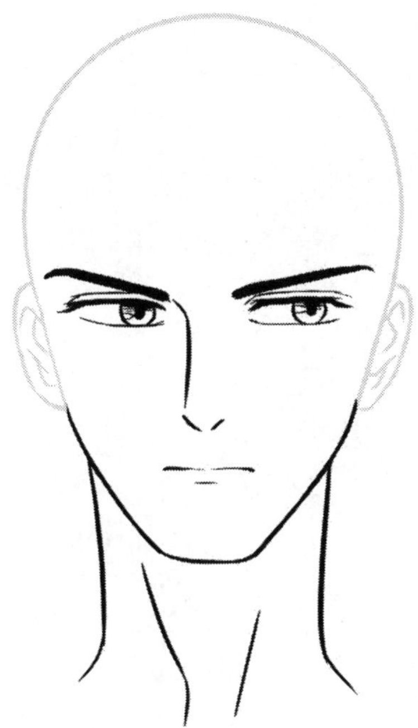

Hairstyle 17:
Spiky Fauxhawk

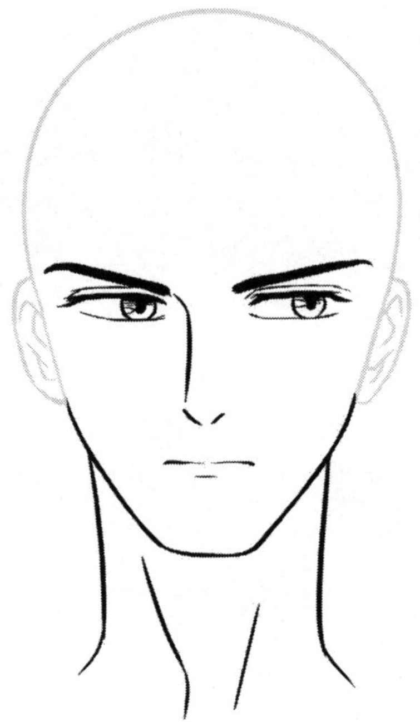

Hairstyle 18:
Classic Short Hair

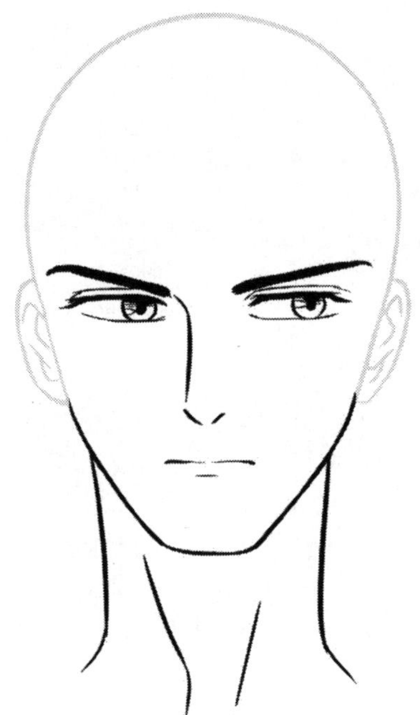

Hairstyle 19:
Short + Wavy

DESIGN YOUR HAIR WORKBOOK: Male (Front)
by Mei Yu

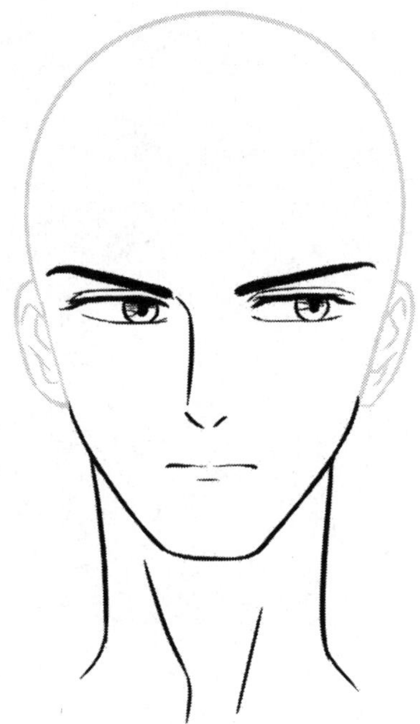

Hairstyle 20:
Edgy Spikes

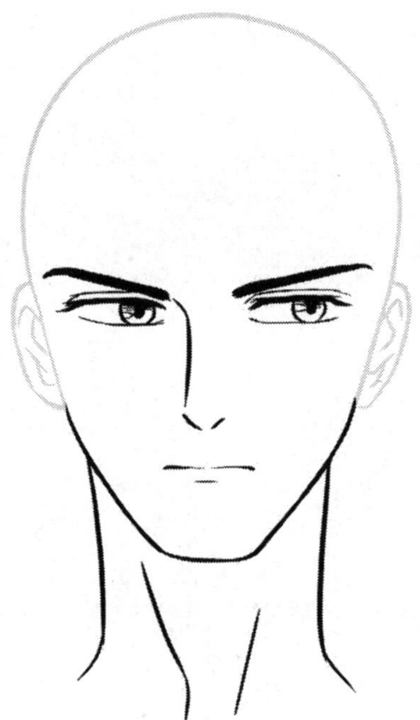

DESIGN YOUR HAIR WORKBOOK: Male (Front)
by Mei Yu

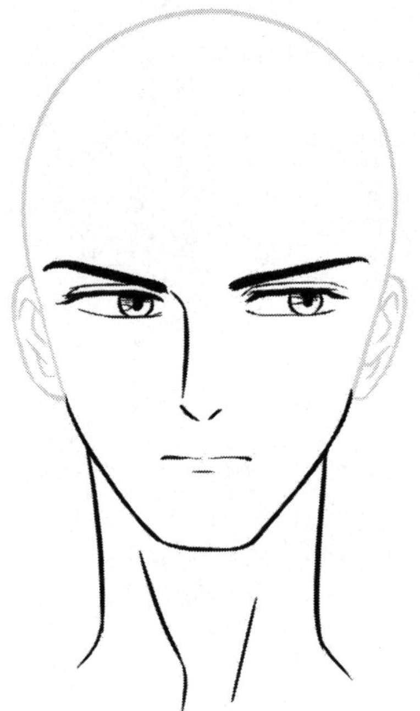

Bonus Template 2

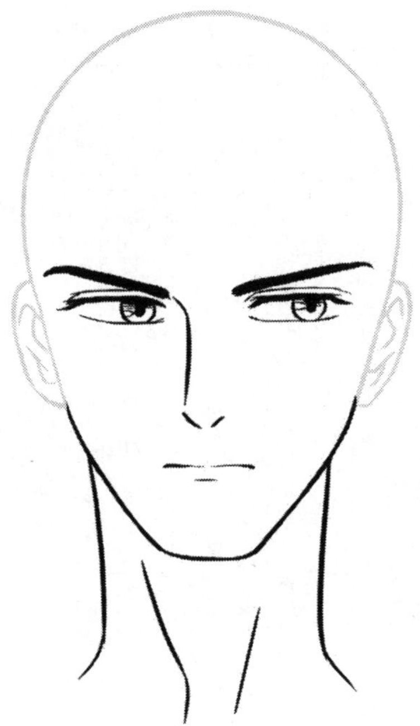

DESIGN YOUR HAIR WORKBOOK: Male (Front)
by Mei Yu

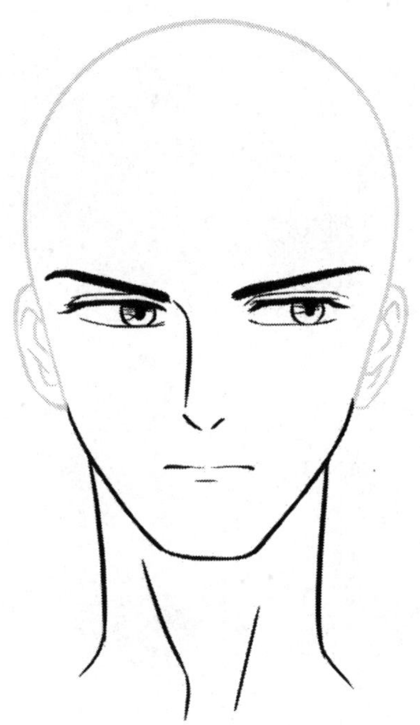

DESIGN YOUR HAIR WORKBOOK: Male (Front)
by Mei Yu

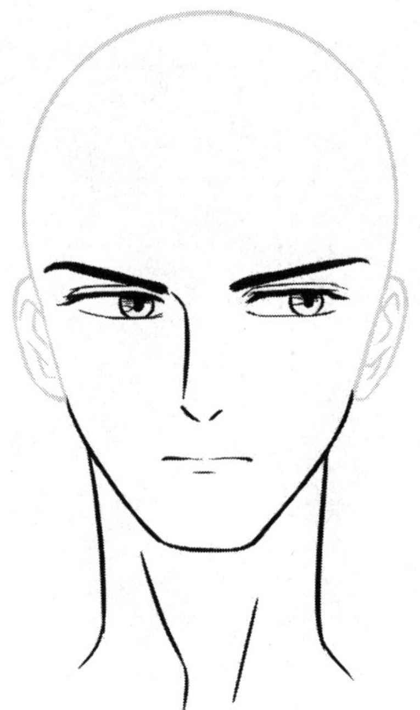

Bonus Template 5

DESIGN YOUR HAIR WORKBOOK: Male (Front)
by Mei Yu

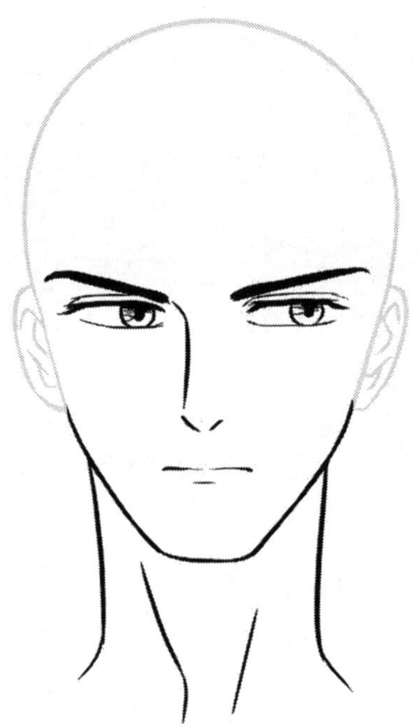

Bonus Template 6

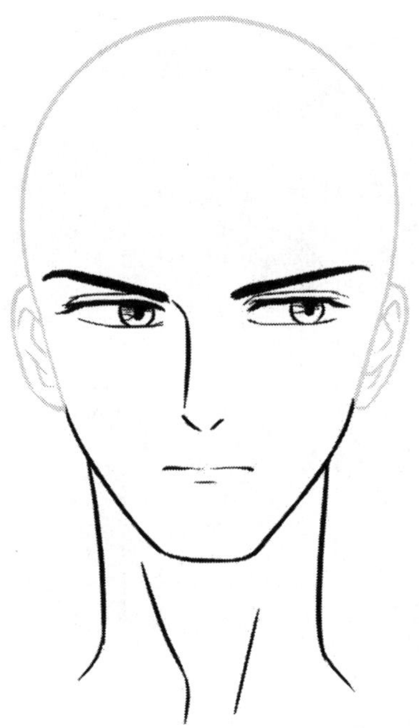

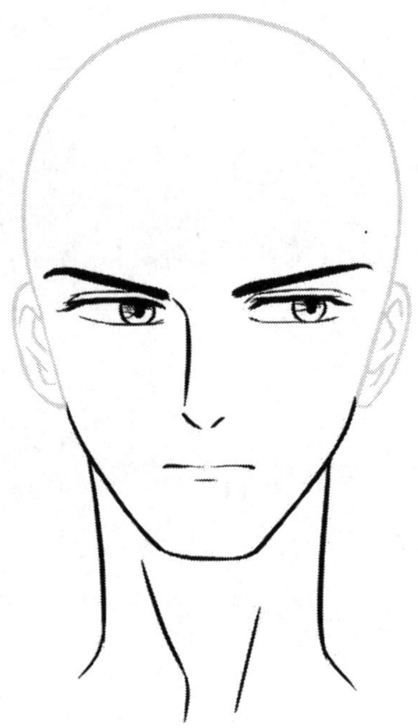

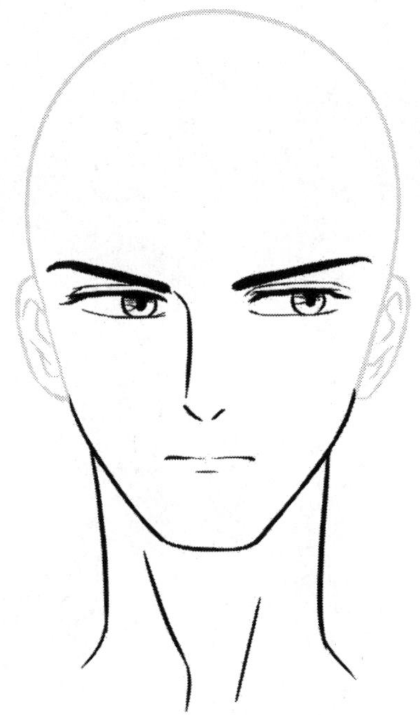

DESIGN YOUR HAIR WORKBOOK: Male (Front)
by Mei Yu

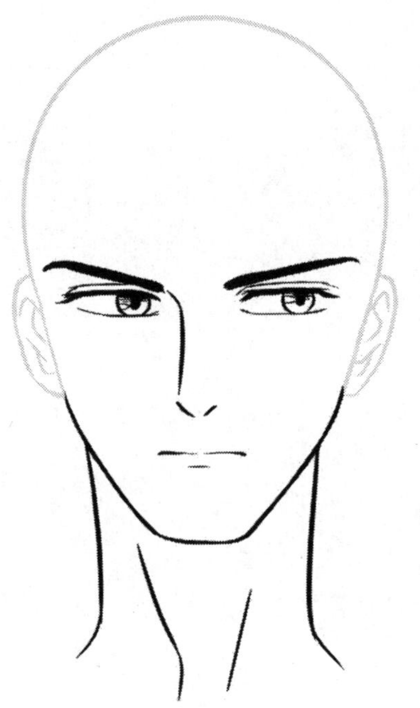

I'm glad you own this WorkBook
to help improve your skills!

I hope you had fun designing, drawing, and
coloring different hairstyles!

If you enjoyed this, please rate and review this WorkBook
on the Amazon page. You can also post some of your
drawings with your review to share.

Your feedback and thoughts can help
others. Thank you very much for your
help and support!

NEW RELEASES - Full Color Books:

Uplifting, Charming Story Book

Inspiring Comic Collection

Art Book

Get inspired by Mei Yu's stories, comics, + art!

Own or Gift!

itunes.apple.com/us/author/mei-yu/id1055789735

available at

www.amazon.com/shop/MeiYu

Android users: Download the Kindle App to get my eBooks

Mei Yu 🔍

Search Amazon, Kindle, & iTunes

DRAW 1 IN 20 EBOOKS

DESIGN YOUR WORKBOOKS

YOU Draw + Color on Templates

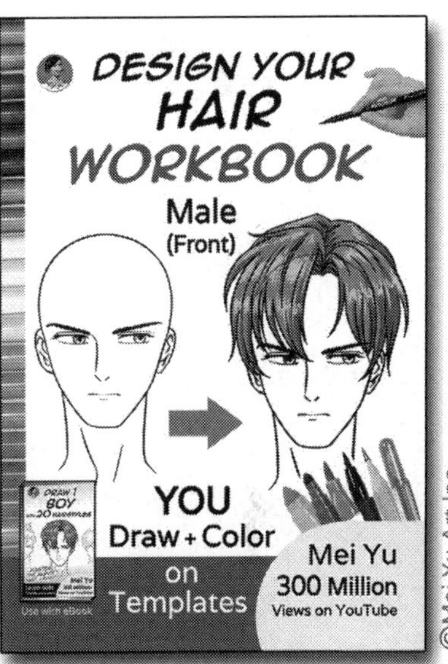

NEW RELEASES

©Mei Yu Art Inc.

★ For doodlers, Manga + comic artists, designers, + aspiring artists

★ Works great with Mei Yu's corresponding eBooks!

★ Draw with pencils, gel pens, markers, colored pencils, & crayons!

available at

amazon

www.amazon.com/shop/meiyu

| Mei Yu WorkBook | 🔍 |

Ships to 100+ countries

Draw Awesome Characters
with Mei Yu's eBooks!

New Release

Learn Skills - Create Your Own Characters!

itunes.apple.com/us/author/mei-yu/id1055789735

available at
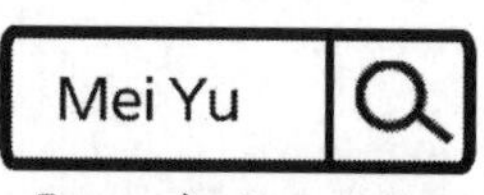

www.amazon.com/shop/MeiYu

Android users: Download the Kindle App to get my eBooks

Mei Yu 🔍

Search Amazon,
Kindle, & iTunes

Learn different styles from
anime · animations · cartoons · games!

Learn other art styles to create your own!

Get it on iBooks — itunes.apple.com/us/author/mei-yu/id1055789735

available at amazon — www.amazon.com/shop/MeiYu

Android users: Download the Kindle App to get my eBooks

Mei Yu 🔍
Search Amazon, Kindle, & iTunes

Mei Yu's APP
DRAW 50
ANIME MANGA LESSONS

2 Collections inside

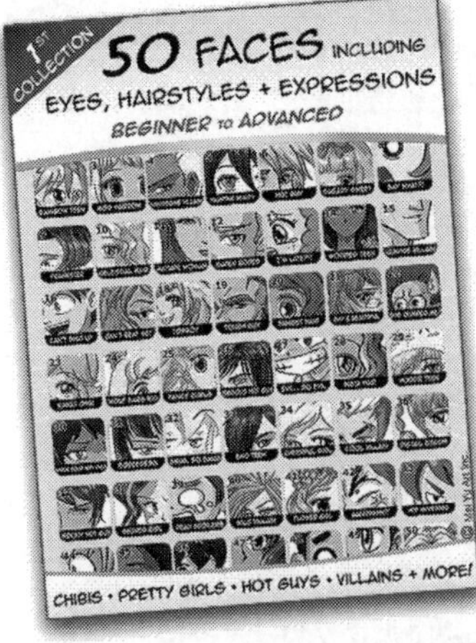

Download on the App Store

Download Now + Draw Better Today!

https://apps.apple.com/developer/mei-yu/id674269351

Mei Yu 🔍

 About Mei Yu

Mei Yu started drawing on walls at age 2. She is a diverse artist, illustrator, and designer from Canada.

Mei also has a popular art channel on YouTube at www.youtube.com/MeiYu with over 1.5 million subscribers, 800 videos, and 300 million views.

Mei has created numerous series of well-loved how to draw eBooks, as well as Coloring Books and Art Books, with the help of her brother.

Since 2004, Mei has been teaching kids and teens her popular anime and cartoon lessons in schools and libraries in North America. Mei continues to inform, entertain, and inspire youth with her beautiful artwork, positive attitude, and cheerful personality.

Mei working on her "100 Paint" video for her fans.

Many of Mei's fans have told her that her art, videos, and books have ignited their passion for art and creativity. Now, many of them have decided to further their art education and pursue their dreams in art, comics, fashion, and design.

Throughout the years, many parents, teachers, and librarians have told Mei that they love her art.

Mei is constantly creating more books, eBooks, and other projects for her fans and readers. She loves sharing her artistic journey with them through her creations.

The more you draw, the better you draw!
Keep up the good work!

Made in United States
Orlando, FL
02 December 2024

54864473R00041